Basic
French

ISBN: 978-1-897457-93-1

Copyright © 2013 Popular Book Company (Canada) Limited

Printed in China

ISBN: 978-1-897457-93-1

Basic French

ISBN: 978-1-897457-93-1

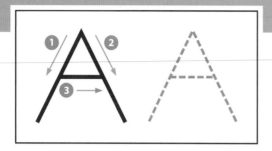

Circle the things that begin with Aa.

l'abricot
apricot

le nid
nest

l'avion
plane

l'abeille
bee

l'arbre
tree

l'araignée
spider

le lapin
rabbit

ISBN: 978-1-897457-93-1

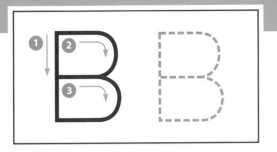

Draw lines to give the baby the things that begin with Bb.

la bavette
bib

le biberon
bottle

la banane
banana

le bébé
baby

le hochet
rattle

ISBN: 978-1-897457-93-1

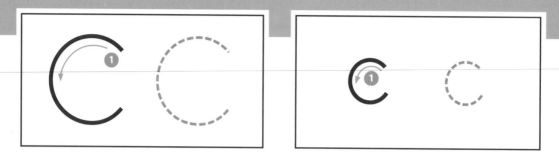

Draw lines to get the animals that begin with Cc to the countryside.

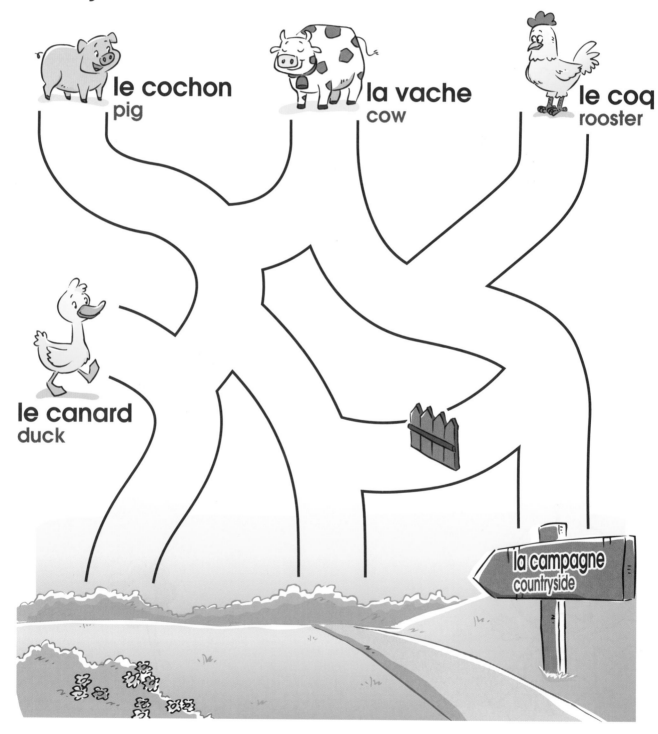

ISBN: 978-1-897457-93-1

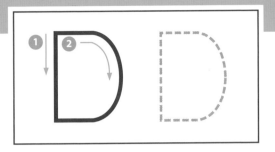
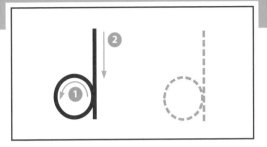

Check ✔ the things that begin with Dd.

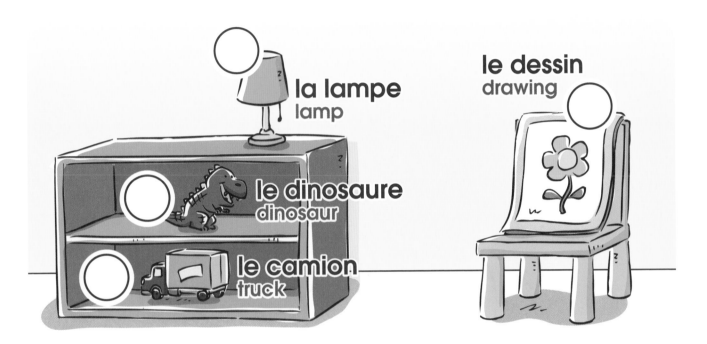

la lampe
lamp

le dinosaure
dinosaur

le camion
truck

le dessin
drawing

le chien
dog

les dames
checkers

ISBN: 978-1-897457-93-1

Trace the word. Then colour that animal in the picture.

l' é é p h a n t

elephant

ISBN: 978-1-897457-93-1

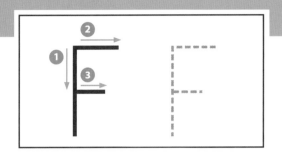
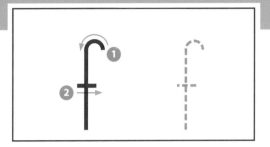

Colour the flowers with Ff.

la fée
fairy

les fleurs
flowers

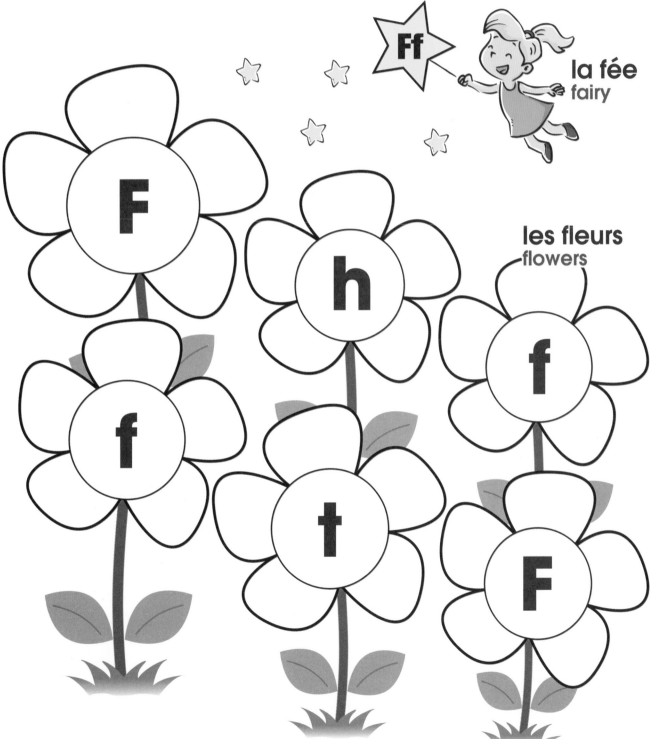

ISBN: 978-1-897457-93-1

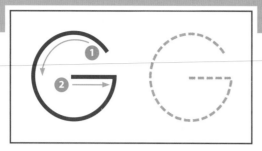
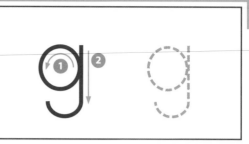

Draw lines to put the food items that begin with Gg on the boy's plate.

le bonbon
candy

la crème glacée
ice cream

la gaufre
waffle

la galette
(a kind of flat cake)

le gâteau
cake

le garçon
boy

ISBN: 978-1-897457-93-1

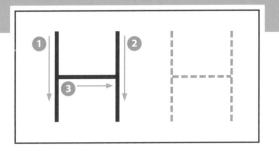
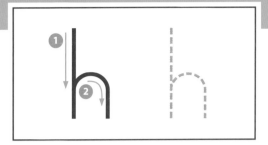

Help the children complete their costumes by drawing lines to their props. Then lead them to the haunted house.

L'Halloween

la harpe
harp

le hochet
rattle

la hache
axe

la maison hantée
haunted house

ISBN: 978-1-897457-93-1

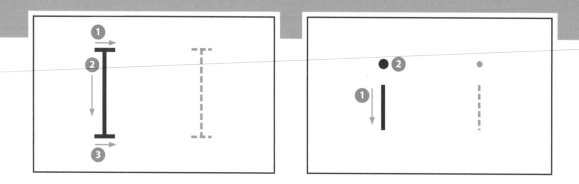

Colour the ice blocks with Ii.

l'igloo
igloo

ISBN: 978-1-897457-93-1

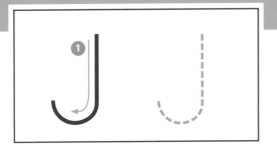 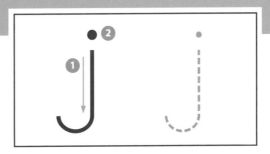

Colour the flower that begins with Jj yellow.

le jardin
garden

la tulipe
tulip

la jonquille
daffodil

la marguerite
daisy

la rose
rose

ISBN: 978-1-897457-93-1

Basic French 13

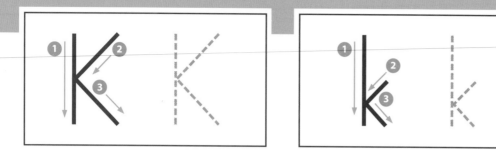

Baby Koala wants to play with Little Kangaroo. Colour the kiwis with Kk to lead Baby Koala to Little Kangaroo.

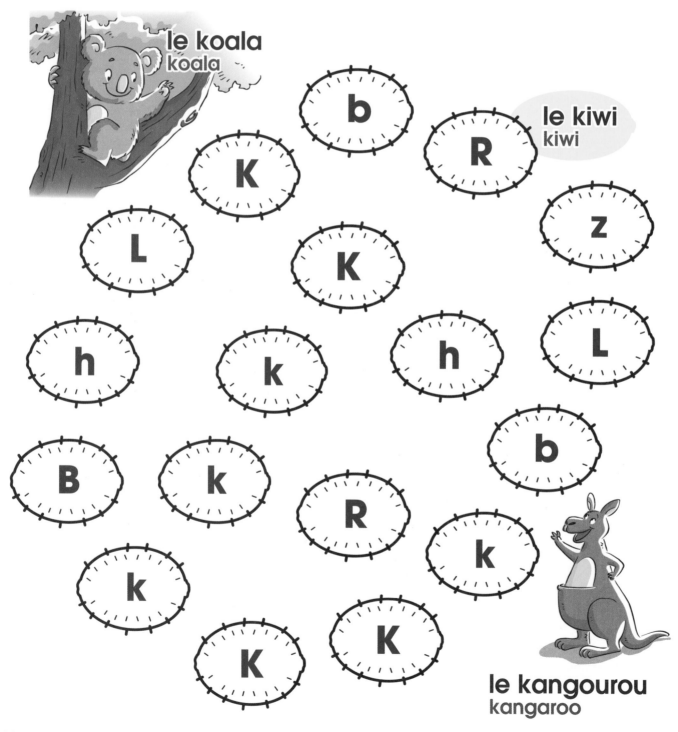

le koala
koala

le kiwi
kiwi

le kangourou
kangaroo

ISBN: 978-1-897457-93-1

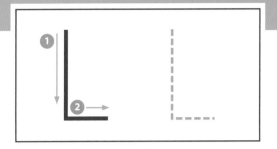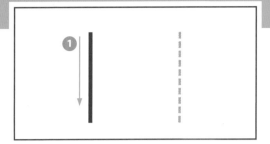

Trace the names of the animals.

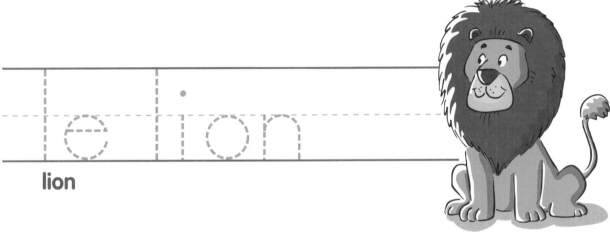
lion

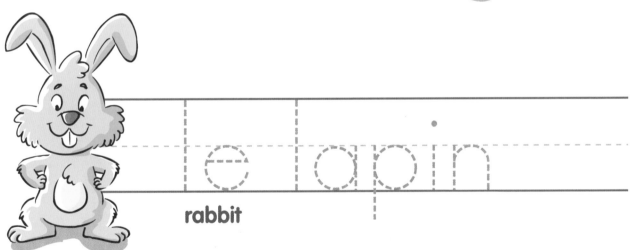
rabbit

lizard

ISBN: 978-1-897457-93-1

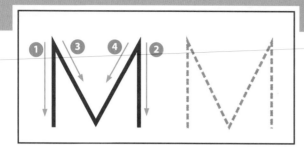

Colour the fruits that begin with **Mm**.

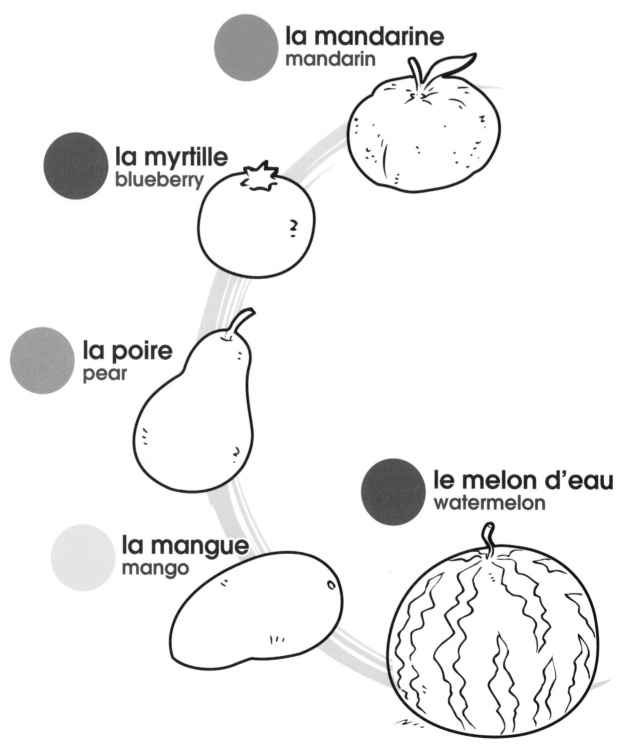

la mandarine
mandarin

la myrtille
blueberry

la poire
pear

le melon d'eau
watermelon

la mangue
mango

ISBN: 978-1-897457-93-1

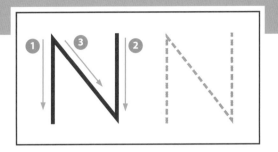
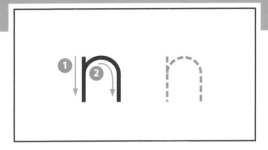

Check ✔ the things that begin with Nn.

Draw the missing picture.

les nuages
clouds

le cobra
cobra

le navet
turnip

la méduse
jellyfish

le navire
ship

ISBN: 978-1-897457-93-1

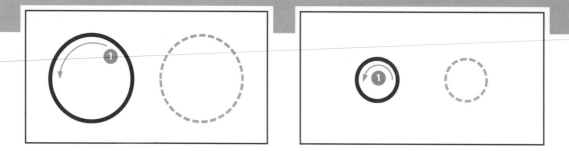

Trace the dotted lines to complete the picture. Then colour the picture.

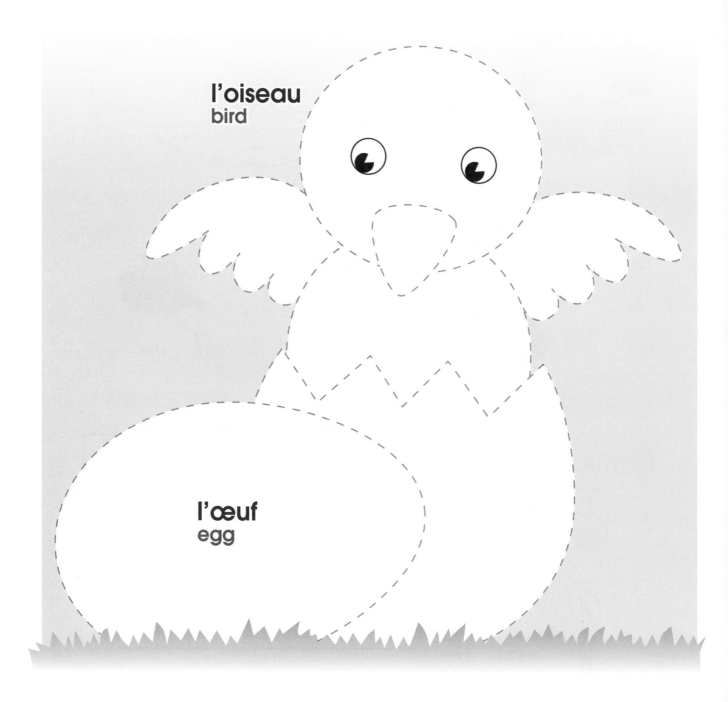

l'oiseau
bird

l'œuf
egg

ISBN: 978-1-897457-93-1

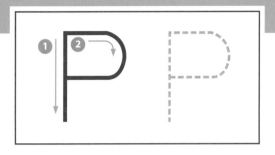

Draw lines to put the things that begin with Pp in Pierre's basket.

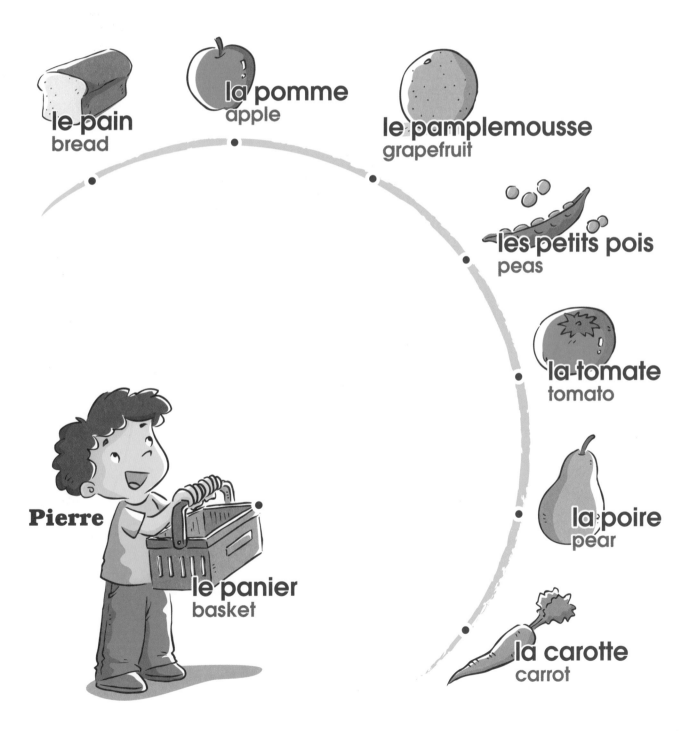

le pain
bread

la pomme
apple

le pamplemousse
grapefruit

les petits pois
peas

la tomate
tomato

Pierre

le panier
basket

la poire
pear

la carotte
carrot

ISBN: 978-1-897457-93-1

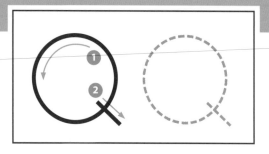 

Help Quentin colour the four bowling pins with Qq. Then trace the words.

quatre quilles

four bowling pins

ISBN: 978-1-897457-93-1

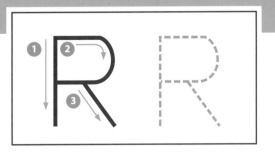

Cross out the things that do not begin with Rr.

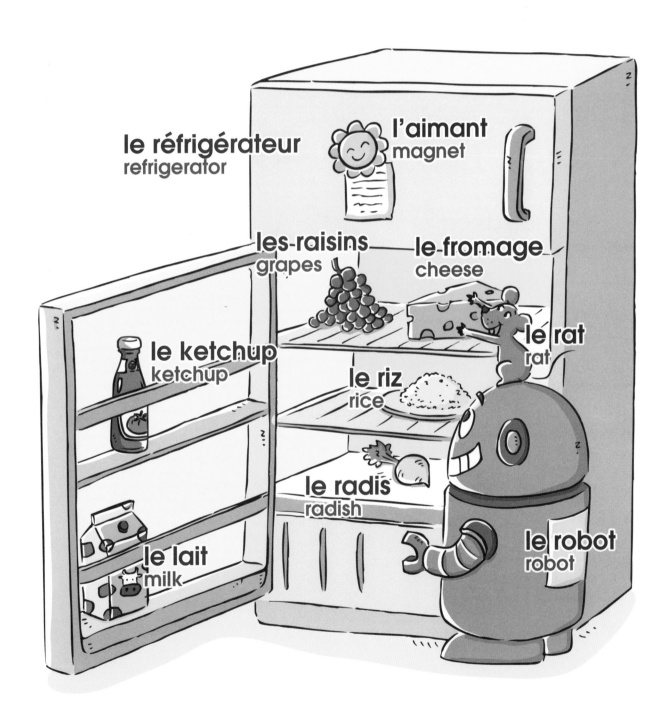

le réfrigérateur
refrigerator

l'aimant
magnet

les-raisins
grapes

le-fromage
cheese

le ketchup
ketchup

le riz
rice

le rat
rat

le radis
radish

le lait
milk

le robot
robot

ISBN: 978-1-897457-93-1

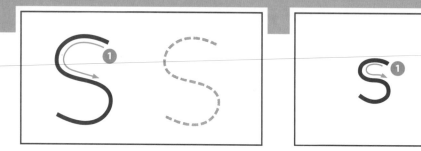

Help Little Mermaid get to the water's surface by colouring the bubbles with things that begin with Ss.

le soleil
sun

le savon
soap

l'os
bone

la fleur
flower

le maïs
corn

le short
shorts

la sirène
mermaid

le seau
pail

le stylo
pen

ISBN: 978-1-897457-93-1

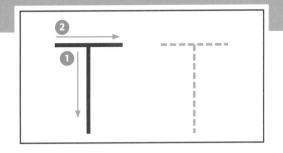
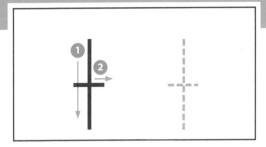

Circle the things that begin with Tt.

le train
train

le tigre
tiger

le papillon
butterfly

la tomate
tomato

la tortue
turtle

le ballon
ball

le panda
panda

la tulipe
tulip

la tasse
cup

ISBN: 978-1-897457-93-1

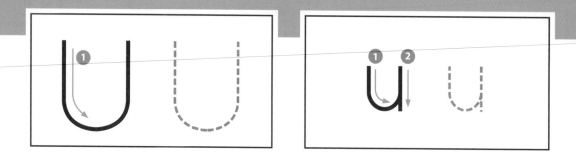

Colour the smoke clouds with Uu. Then trace the words.

a factory

ISBN: 978-1-897457-93-1

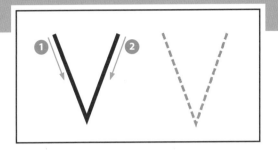 

Trace the lines to put the things that begin with Vv in the trunk of the car.

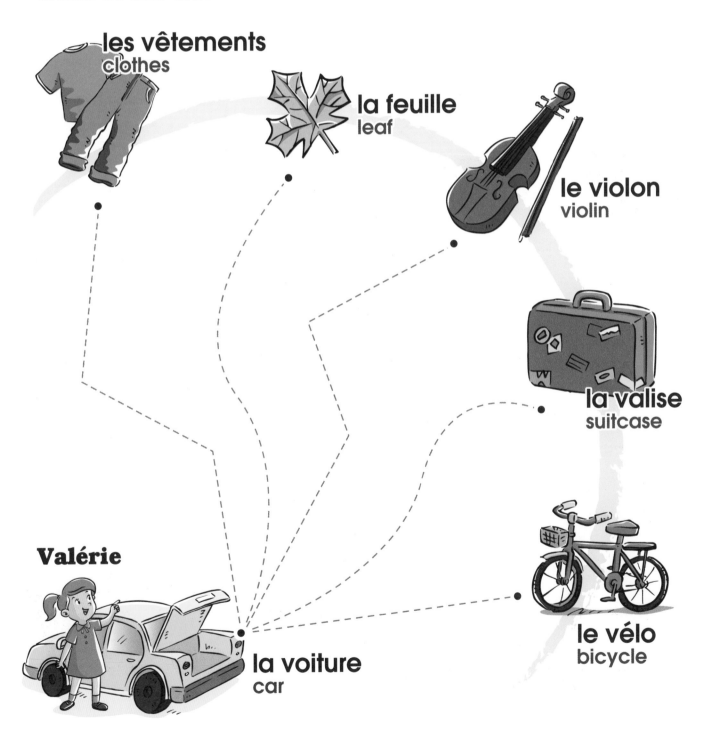

les vêtements
clothes

la feuille
leaf

le violon
violin

la valise
suitcase

Valérie

la voiture
car

le vélo
bicycle

ISBN: 978-1-897457-93-1

Colour the arrows with Ww to help William find his lost wagon.

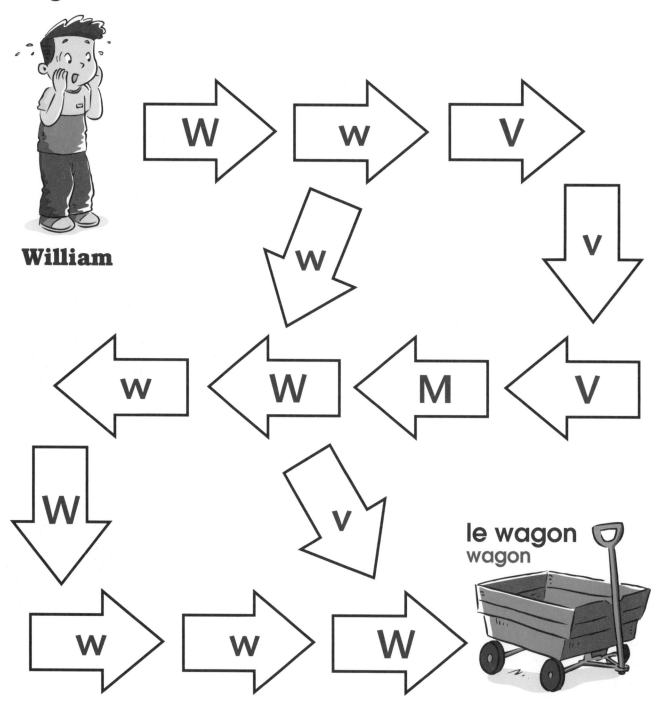

William

le wagon
wagon

ISBN: 978-1-897457-93-1

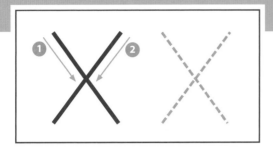
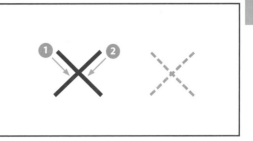

Colour the xylophone. Then trace the words.

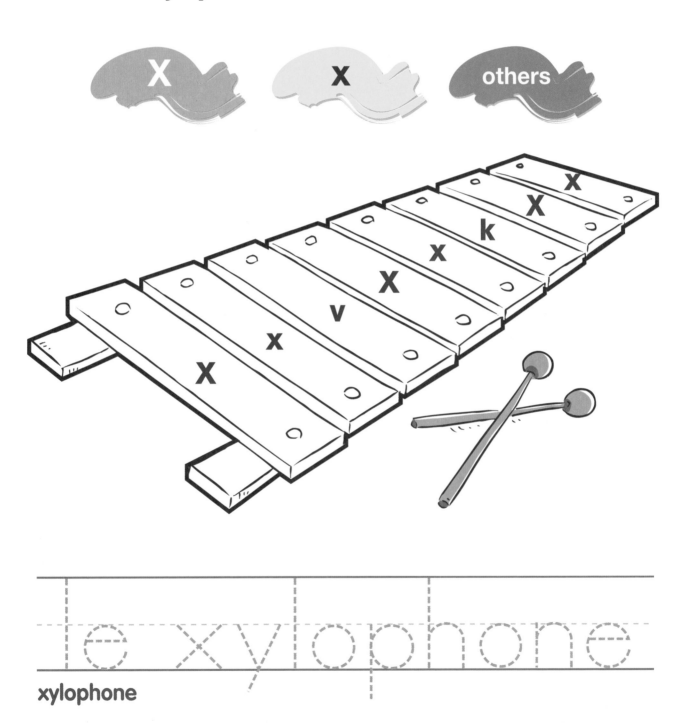

xylophone

ISBN: 978-1-897457-93-1

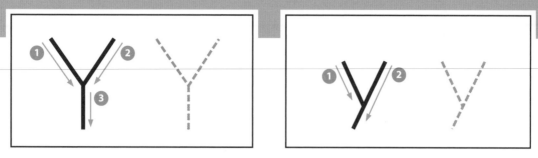

Trace the letter Yy. Then draw the yo-yo Yves is playing with.

le yo-yo
yo-yo

Yves

ISBN: 978-1-897457-93-1

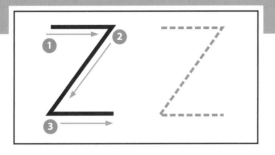

Little Zebra wants to get back to the zoo. Help him by tracing the zigzag.

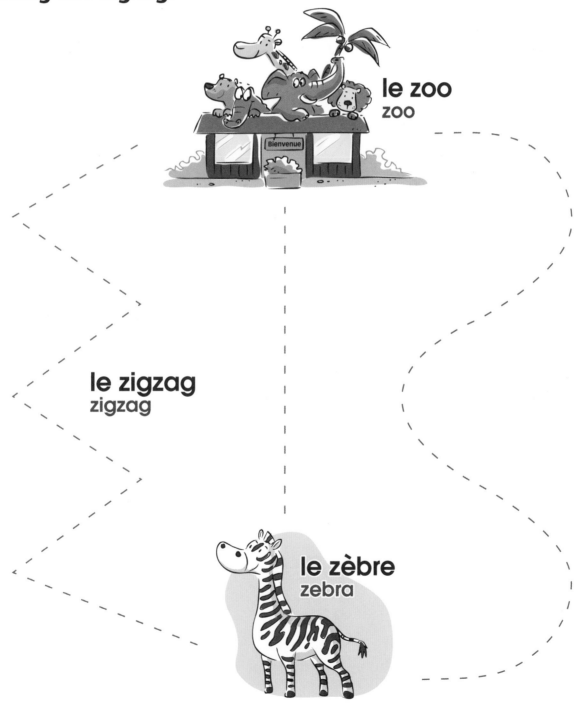

le zoo
zoo

le zigzag
zigzag

le zèbre
zebra

ISBN: 978-1-897457-93-1

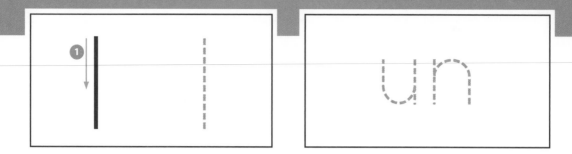

Colour the balloons that have 1 star on them.

un
one

ISBN: 978-1-897457-93-1

Trace the lines to put the objects in pairs in the basket.

deux
two

ISBN: 978-1-897457-93-1

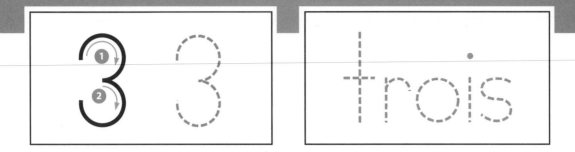

Draw 3 scoops of ice cream. Write the word for 3.

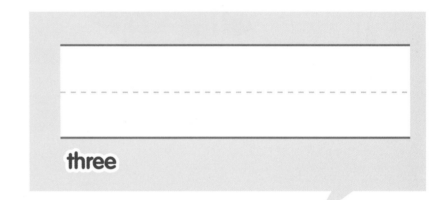

three

trois
three

ISBN: 978-1-897457-93-1

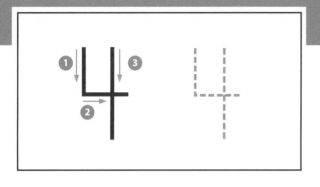

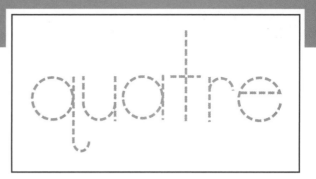

Draw the correct number of candles to show how old Jazzy is.

quatre ans
four years old

Bonne fête, Jazzy!

ISBN: 978-1-897457-93-1

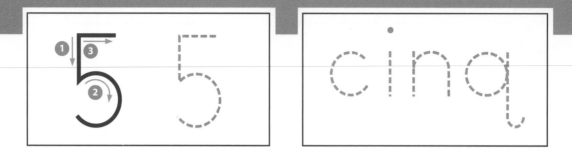

Trace and write the word for 5. Then draw lines to groups of 5.

five

ISBN: 978-1-897457-93-1

Colour the balls that represent 6.

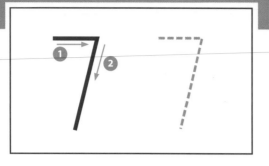

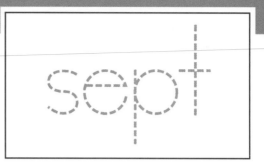

Colour the number of bones Little Puppy wants.

sept
seven

ISBN: 978-1-897457-93-1

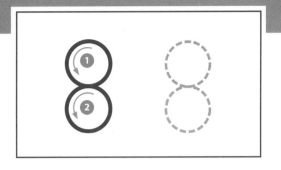
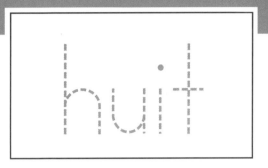

Draw 8 chocolate chips on the cookie.

huit
eight

ISBN: 978-1-897457-93-1

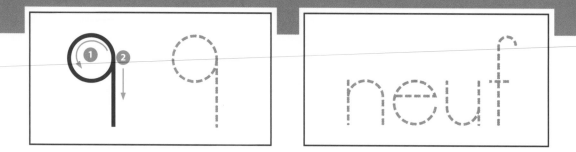

Trace the number and the word. Then colour the bunches that have 9 grapes.

nine

ISBN: 978-1-897457-93-1

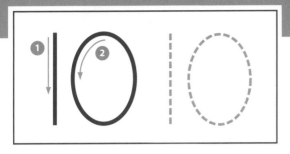 

Trace the word. Then colour the stars with 10 on them.

dix

ten

ISBN: 978-1-897457-93-1

Help Rousse collect the red apples by colouring the ones with the word "rouge" on them red. Then draw lines to put them in the basket.

rouge
red

ISBN: 978-1-897457-93-1

Trace and colour the carrot orange.

orange
orange

ISBN: 978-1-897457-93-1

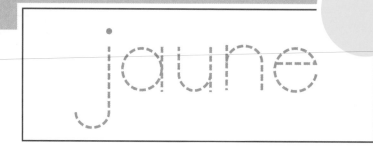

For the vases with the word "jaune", colour their flowers yellow.

jaune
yellow

jaune

rose

jaune

ISBN: 978-1-897457-93-1

vert

Check ✔ the green vegetables.

Help Bernard catch four fish with letters that form the word "bleu". Colour these fish blue and draw lines to connect them to the hook.

bleu
blue

 ISBN: 978-1-897457-93-1

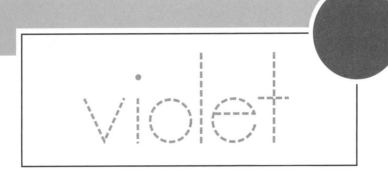

Colour the girl's clothing purple.

violet
purple

Help Mother Brown Bear find her baby. Colour her path brown.

ISBN: 978-1-897457-93-1

rose

Circle the pink butterflies. Then colour the girl's dress pink.

rose
pink

ISBN: 978-1-897457-93-1

noir

Draw black patches on the cow.

noir
black

ISBN: 978-1-897457-93-1

blanc

Add smiles to the white ghosts.

Trace and colour the circles to complete the picture.

les cercles
circles

ISBN: 978-1-897457-93-1

carré

Carel likes square crackers. Trace and colour the square crackers for him.

les carrés
squares

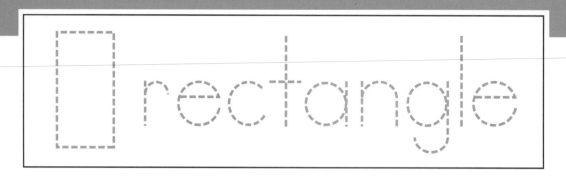

Help Renée collect the presents in the shape of rectangles as she goes to her birthday party. Colour her path.

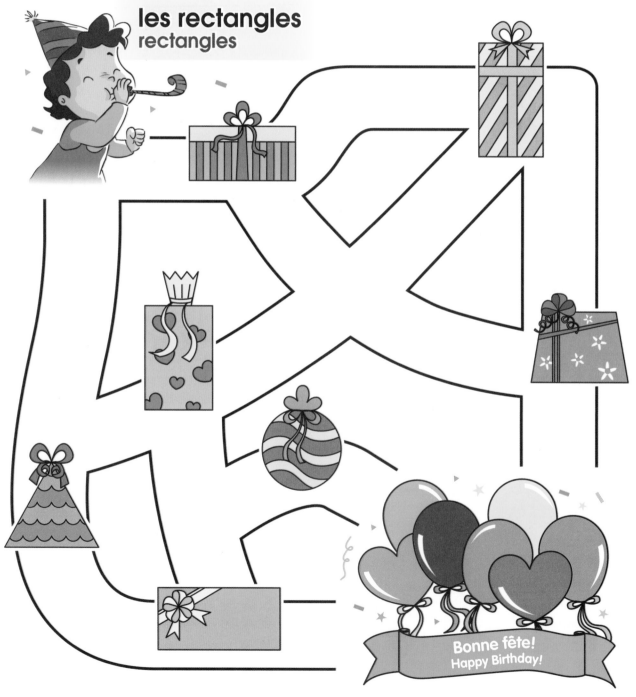

les rectangles
rectangles

Bonne fête!
Happy Birthday!

ISBN: 978-1-897457-93-1

△ triangle

Circle the things with triangles.

les triangles
triangles

The children are flying kites in the shape of diamonds. Draw lines to connect the children with their kites.

les losanges
diamonds

ISBN: 978-1-897457-93-1

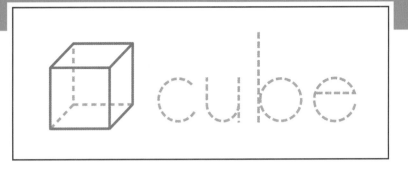

Trace the cube. Then paste or draw a picture of an object that looks like a cube.

les **cubes**
cubes

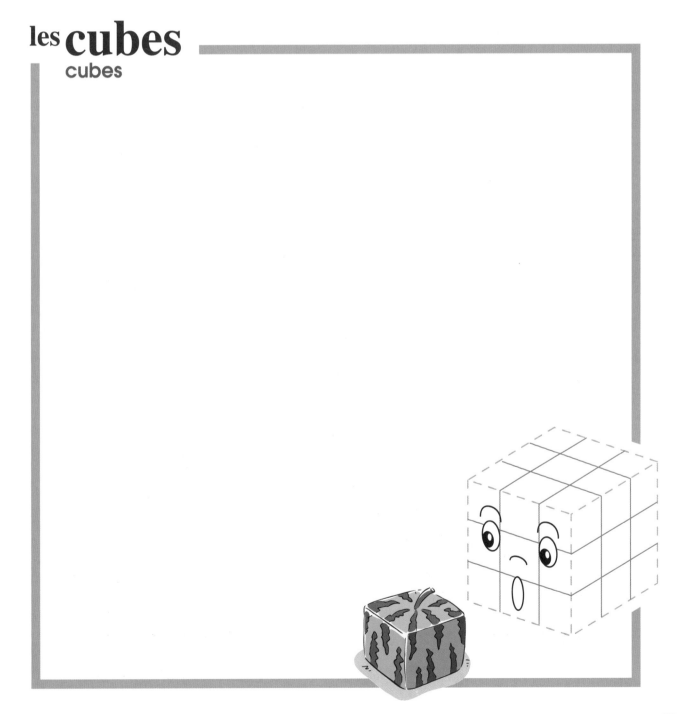

ISBN: 978-1-897457-93-1

Colour the things that look like cones.

les cônes
cones

ISBN: 978-1-897457-93-1

Help Selena trace the lines to thread only the sphere-shaped beads. Then colour those beads.

les sphères
spheres

ISBN: 978-1-897457-93-1

Connect each shape with an object that begins with the same letter.

ISBN: 978-1-897457-93-1

Count and circle the correct numbers. Then fill in the missing first letters.

quatre / cinq

[ ]ommes

sept / huit

[ ]leurs

deux / trois

[ ]anards

ISBN: 978-1-897457-93-1

Colour the crayons. Then colour the shapes in the picture.

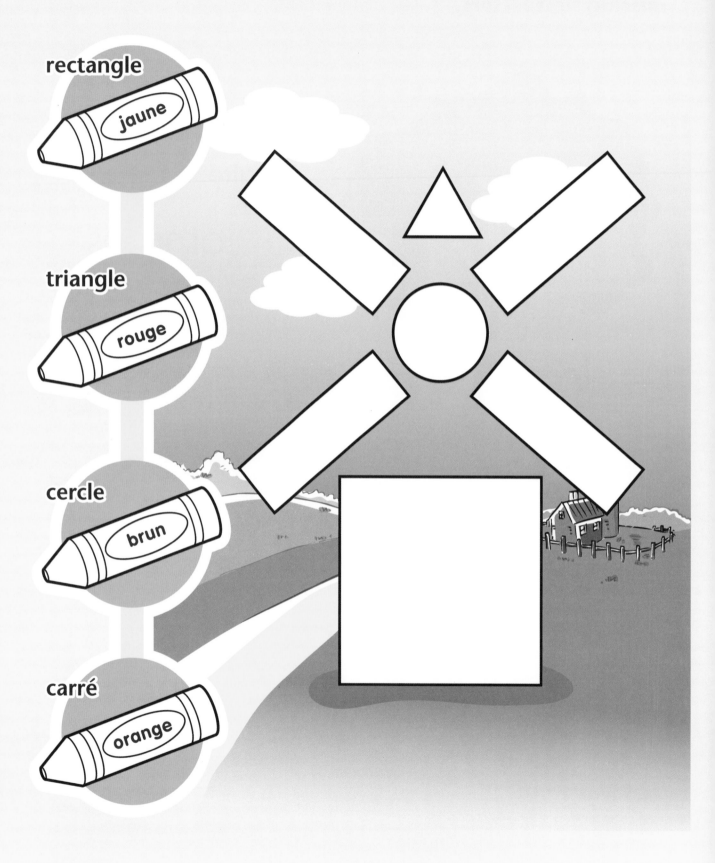

rectangle
jaune

triangle
rouge

cercle
brun

carré
orange

ISBN: 978-1-897457-93-1

Count the solids. Colour and write the number of solids in words. Then circle the correct words.

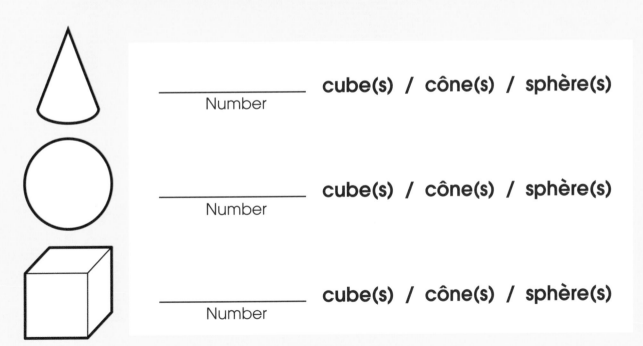

_____ cube(s) / cône(s) / sphère(s)
Number

_____ cube(s) / cône(s) / sphère(s)
Number

_____ cube(s) / cône(s) / sphère(s)
Number

Help the pirate find the treasure chest. Draw a line to show his way.

WAY TO THE **TREASURE**

deux cercles

neuf losanges

quatre carrés

ISBN: 978-1-897457-93-1

Find eight colour words in the word search. Colour the boxes with those colours.

**Draw a picture of an object that looks like each of the solids.
Then write the names of the solids.**

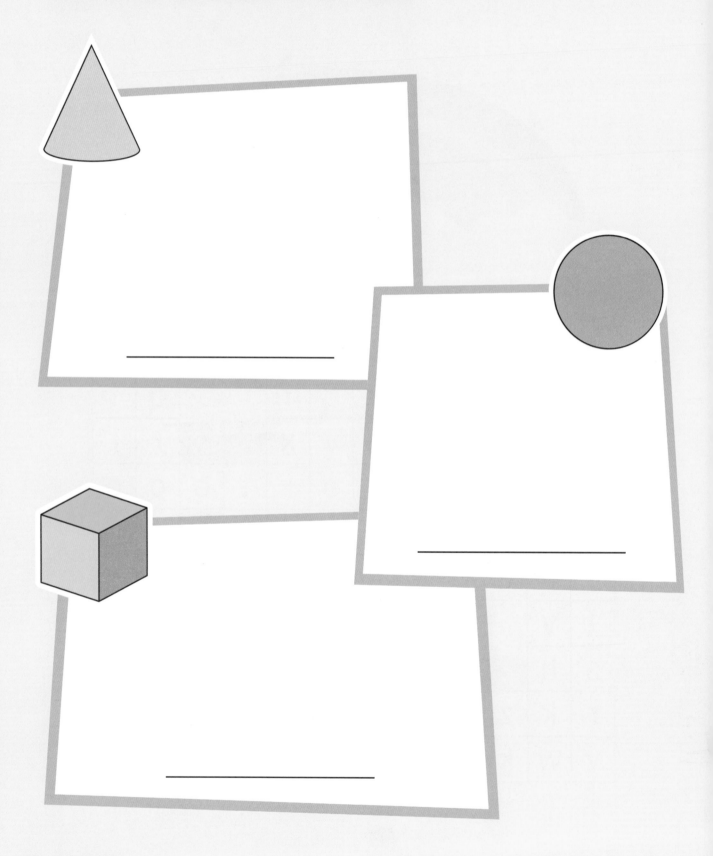

ISBN: 978-1-897457-93-1